WS.

PROJECT

PROJECT

NURSERY

this
little 🌳 o
book bel

· · · · · · · · · · · · · ·

· · · · · · · · · · · · · ·

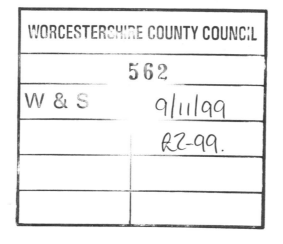

ORCHARD BOOKS
96 Leonard Street, London EC2A 4RH
Orchard Books Australia
14 Mars Road, Lane Cove, NSW 2066
1 86039 666 6 (hardback)
1 86039 743 3 (paperback)
First published in Great Britain in 1998
Copyright © Penny Dann 1998
The right of Penny Dann to be identified as the author and
illustrator of this work has been asserted by her in accordance
with the Copyright, Designs and Patents Act, 1988.
A CIP catalogue record for this book is available from the British Library.
Printed in Italy

Incey Wincey Spider

Penny Dann

little ORCHARD

Incey Wincey Spider ...

climbed up the
water spout.

Down came
the rain ...

and washed poor
Incey out!

Out came
the sunshine

and dried up
all the rain.

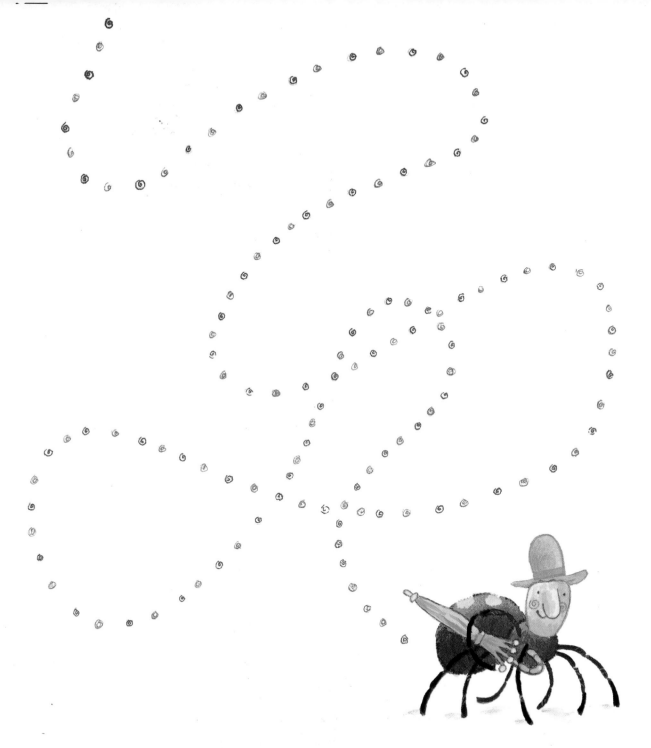

So Incey Wincey
Spider ...

climbed up the
spout again.